DATE DUE

PRINTED IN U.S.A.

The United States

Hawaii

Bob Italia
ABDO & Daughters

visit us at
www.abdopub.com

Published by Abdo & Daughters, 4940 Viking Drive, Suite 622, Edina, Minnesota 55435.
Copyright © 1998 by Abdo Consulting Group, Inc., Pentagon Tower, P.O. Box 36036,
Minneapolis, Minnesota 55435 USA. International copyrights reserved in all countries.
No part of this book may be reproduced in any form without written permission from the
publisher.

Printed in the United States.

Cover and Interior Photo credits: Peter Arnold, Inc., Super Stock

Edited by Lori Kinstad Pupeza
Contributing editor Brooke Henderson
Special thanks to our Checkerboard Kids—Morgan Roberts, Annie O'Leary, Aisha Baker,
Jack Ward

All statistics taken from the 1990 census; The Rand McNally Discovery Atlas of The
United States. Other sources: Compton's Encyclopedia, 1997; *Hawaii*, Heinrichs,
Children's Press, Chicago, 1989.

Library of Congress Cataloging-in-Publication Data

Italia, Bob, 1955-
      Hawaii / Bob Italia.
      p. cm. -- (The United States)
      Includes Index.
      Summary: Examines the geography, history, natural resources, people, and
      recreational activities of Hawaii.
      ISBN 1-56239-856-3
      1. Hawaii--Juvenile literature. [1. Hawaii.] I. Title. II. Series: United States
      (Series)
      DU623.25.I83 1998
      996.9--dc21   97-11224
                                                            CIP
                                                             AC

Contents

Welcome to Hawaii

Hawaii is the newest state to become part of the United States. It is made up of **volcanic** islands in the mid-Pacific Ocean. Hawaii is called the Aloha State. Aloha means hello and good bye in the Hawaiian language.

Hawaii was first settled long ago by people from the island of Tahiti. The first Europeans to visit the islands were Captain James Cook, a British naval officer, and his crews in 1778. Later, Hawaii became famous for its pineapple and sugarcane crops.

Americans entered World War II because of a surprise Japanese attack (Dec. 7, 1941) on the U.S. military in Pearl Harbor. Hawaii became the 50th state on August 21, 1959. Now it is a popular vacation spot for people all over the world.

Waterfall on Pali Coast, Kauai, Hawaii.

Fast Facts

HAWAII

Capital and largest city
Honolulu (365,272 people)
Area
6,427 square miles
(16,646 sq km)
Population
1,115,274 people
Rank: 40th
Statehood
August 21, 1959
(50th state admitted)
Highest point
Mauna Kea; 13,796 feet
(4,205 m), on Hawaii
Motto
Ua mau ke ea o ka aina i ka pono
(The life of the land is
perpetuated in righteousness)
Song
"Hawaii Ponoi"
Famous People
Don Ho, Daniel K. Inouye, King
Kamehameha, and Bette Midler.

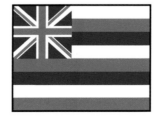

*S*tate Flag

*H*ibiscus

*H*awaiian Goose

*C*andlenut

About Hawaii
The Aloha State

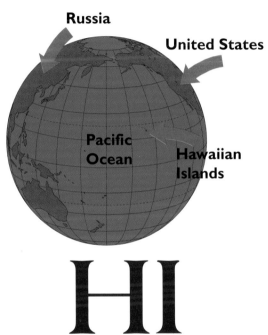

Detail area

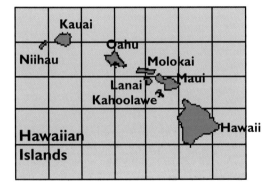

Kauai
Niihau
Oahu
Molokai
Maui
Lanai
Kahoolawe
Hawaii
Hawaiian Islands

Russia
United States
Pacific Ocean
Hawaiian Islands

HI
Hawaii's abbreviation

Borders: The Hawaiian Islands are bordered on all sides by the Pacific Ocean.

Nature's Treasures

Half the state is covered with **tropical** forests. Common trees are koa, lehua, guava, and screw pine. Almost 1,400 kinds of flowers and plants grow in Hawaii, including orchids, hibiscus, gardenias, and poinsettias.

Because the islands are in the middle of the Pacific Ocean, few land **mammals** have come to Hawaii. Bats, birds, lizards, insects, and seals were the only land creatures on the islands when the **Polynesians** came. They brought with them dogs, pigs, and rats. Cats, horses, cattle, goats, and sheep were brought to the islands by Europeans. Marlin, dolphin, and tuna can be found swimming in the ocean.

The state has few important **minerals**. Bauxite is found on Kauai. There are large amounts of limestone, sand, gravel, stone, and clay. There are many streams and waterfalls, but rain water is collected for watering. Pineapple and sugarcane were also brought to the islands. They are still grown on the islands, along with papaya and guava.

Hawaii's weather is one of its greatest treasures. Its warm temperatures change little from night to day or from month to month. The sun often shines on the islands, but they do get their fair share of rain. Mount Waialeale on Kauai is one of the wettest places on Earth. It gets about 480 inches (12,192 mm) of rain every year.

hibiscus flower

Beginnings

The Hawaiian Islands were made by volcanoes 25 million years ago. Between the years A.D. 300 and 900, **Polynesians** from the Marquesas Islands and Tahiti lived on some of the Hawaiian Islands. These brave people traveled across the Pacific Ocean in large canoes. They made tools and built homes, and they enjoyed a good life on Hawaii.

The first Europeans to see the islands were the British party of Captain James Cook. Cook landed on Kauai in January 1778. He named the islands the Sandwich Islands, in honor of the fourth earl of Sandwich, head of the British Army. Cook was killed by Hawaiians in 1779. But foreigners soon began trading with the islanders.

One island ruler, Kamehameha I, took over the Hawaii Island in a 10 year war (1782-1792). By 1810,

he ruled all the main islands. Kamehameha's success came from his use of guns bought from white people.

In 1820, **missionaries** arrived from New England. By the mid-1800s, Hawaii built whaling ships, more than any other state, for America. In the late 1800s, sugarcane **plantations** were started. Workers were brought from east Asia to work on them.

In 1893, Queen Liliuokalani was **dethroned**. Not long after this happened, the Republic of Hawaii was created. Pineapples and sugarcane had become major crops.

The United States built a large military base at Pearl Harbor in 1911. America entered World War II after a surprise Japanese attack on Pearl Harbor. After the war, the Hawaiian islands became a popular vacation spot. Hawaii became the 50th state on August 21, 1959. Since then, **tourism** has become the leading **industry**.

B.C. to 1800

New Arrivals

300-900: Some of the islands are settled by **Polynesians**, who come in large canoes.

1778: Captain James Cook arrives on the islands and names them the Sandwich Islands after his sponsor, England's earl of Sandwich. He is killed by Hawaiians on his return trip in 1779.

1795: Chief Kamehameha conquers most of the islands and unifies them. His kingdom lasts until 1893.

Hawaii
B.C. to 1800

1819 to 1900

Settlements of Hawaii

1819: The first American whaling ships arrive in Honolulu. Whaling reaches its peak in 1858.

1820: The first New England **missionaries** arrive and establish schools.

1835: The first sugarcane plantation is formed on Kauai.

1886: The pineapple **industry** makes its first appearance on the islands.

1893: Queen Liliuokalani is **dethroned**, and a new government is started.

Hawaii

1819 to 1900

1911 to Now

Hawaii Joins the Union

 1911: The United States Military builds a large base at Pearl Harbor near Honolulu.

 1916: Hawaii **Volcanoes** National Park is built.

 1941: The Japanese attack Pearl Harbor; the United States enters World War II.

 1959: Hawaii becomes the 50th state of America.

 1983-1989: The Kilauea Volcano erupts, destroys lots of homes, and forces 400 people to leave the area.

Hawaii
1911 to Now

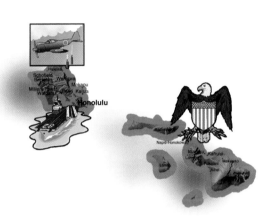

Hawaii's People

Over one million people live in Hawaii. Many live in or near the cities of Honolulu on Oahu, or Hilo on the island of Hawaii (also known as "the Big Island").

Some of its people are white, but most are Asians, including Japanese, Filipino, Hawaiian (descendants of the **Polynesians**), and Chinese. There are also some African Americans, Hispanics, and Native Americans.

Father Damien, a Belgian priest, took charge of a **leper colony** on Molokai in 1873. He helped improve the water, food supplies, and housing. He also started two orphanages. Though he caught **leprosy** in 1885, he refused to leave the island. Hawaii honored his memory in its National Statuary Hall in 1965.

Swimming champion Duke Kahanamoku was born in 1890 near Honolulu. The greatest swimmer of his time, he won the 100 meter freestyle event in the 1912 and 1920 Olympic Games. He became the sheriff of Honolulu from 1932 to 1961.

Actress Bette Midler was also born in Honolulu (1945). She went on to star in *The Rose* (1979), *Beaches* (1988), *Ruthless People* (1986), and other movies. Her song "Wind Beneath My Wings" won a Grammy Award for the best song of the year.

This girl is saying Aloha!

Splendid Cities

The largest cities are Honolulu and Pearl City (both on Oahu). Kailua, Hilo, Aiea, Kaneohe, and Waipahu are other cities. Hilo is on Hawaii, but the rest are on Oahu where most of the population lives.

Honolulu is the capital. Many people live there, more than any other city in Hawaii. It is a busy **port city**, and has the biggest airport in Hawaii. Hilo is the second largest city. It also is a major port, and has an airport. The other main ports are Kahului, on Maui; Kawaihae, on Hawaii island; and Nawiliwili, on Kauai. **Tourists** stay at hotels that tower over Hawaii's cities.

Honolulu, Hawaii, at sunset.

Hawaii's Land

The state of Hawaii is made up of eight islands (from biggest to smallest): Hawaii, Maui, Oahu, Kauai, Molokai, Lanai, Niihau, and Kahoolawe. Lanai and Niihau are privately owned. No one lives on Kahoolawe because the military uses it for target practice.

Hawaii is part of a long volcanic chain of islands in the Pacific Ocean. Every major Hawaiian island was formed by at least one **volcano**. Only the island of Hawaii has active volcanoes.

Most of the islands have **tropical** forests on their jagged highland peaks, and on their eastern and northern shores. Most of the rain falls on those areas. The shorelines are often guarded by steep cliffs that rise up from sand beaches.

Keanae, Maui, Hawaii

Hawaii at Play

Hawaii has many large sand beaches. Many people enjoy surfing, scuba diving, wind surfing, and deep-sea fishing in the Pacific Ocean. Because of Hawaii's beautiful waterfalls, rain forests, and **volcanoes**, people like to hike, camp, and bike.

Besides enjoying Hawaii's beauty, people can experience Honolulu's museums, the **symphony orchestra**, the ballet company, and several theater groups. Hawaiians are known for their graceful hula dance. The ukulele (a stringed instrument) and the steel guitar are popular.

Many of Hawaii's historical sites date from the pre-European period. The Pu'uhonua o Honaunau National Historical Park, on Hawaii island, includes royal fishponds, coconut groves, and beautiful coastal scenery. Puukohola

Heiau National Historic Site, on Hawaii island, is the site of ruins of a royal temple. The U.S.S. Arizona Memorial, at Pearl Harbor, was built in honor of crew members of a ship sunk by the Japanese on December 7, 1941.

Also popular are Haleakala National Park, on Maui, and Hawaii **Volcanoes** National Park, on Hawaii. Diamond Head and Punchbowl, two **extinct** volcanoes, are famous **landmarks** near Honolulu.

Waikiki Beach, Oahu Island.

Hawaii at Work

Tourism is the biggest business on Hawaii. Each year the islands attract a few million visitors. Oahu is the favorite stop. The state's warm climate and its fine sand beaches—especially Waikiki Beach—are main attractions.

Hawaii grows the most sugarcane in the United States. About ten million tons are harvested every year. Most sugarcane is grown on large **plantations** located on Hawaii, Maui, Oahu, and Kauai islands. Hawaii also grows the most pineapples of any state. They are grown on Lanai, Oahu, and Maui. Other crops include coffee, ornamental flowers and shrubs, papayas, bananas, avocados, macadamia nuts, alfalfa, beans, potatoes, and cabbage.

Livestock farms produce beef cows, hogs, chickens, and dairy foods. Large cattle ranches are found on Niihau, Hawaii island, and Maui. Cutting trees for wood is a small **industry**. Most wood is used for buildings, furniture, and crafts.

The fishing industry is small but growing. Yellowfin and skipjack tuna are the main catches. Sport fishing is very popular in Hawaii.

There isn't a lot of mining in Hawaii. There aren't many **minerals** in the earth. The top mineral products are stone, cement, sand, and gravel. Most are used by the state's large construction industry.

Sugarcane fields, Maui, Hawaii.

Fun Facts

•There are eight major islands that make up the state of Hawaii. The island of Hawaii is the largest island. It was formed by five **volcanoes**. Kilauea (4,090 ft high, 1,247 m) and Mauna Loa (13,677 ft high, 4,169 m) are still active.

•Haleakala (10,023 ft high, 3,055 m) on Maui has one of the world's largest **extinct** volcanic craters.

•The highest point is Mauna Kea (13,796 ft high, 4,205 m), an extinct volcano on Hawaii Island.

•There are 132 islands that make up Hawaii, on which only eight are big enough for people to live.

•Surfing was invented long ago in Hawaii by ancient kings.

Opposite page: Haleakala Crater, Maui, Hawaii.

Glossary

Extinct: no longer existing.

Dethroned: when a king or queen has their title or power taken away from them.

Industry: any kind of business.

Landmark: something familiar or easily seen, used as a guide.

Leprosy: a disease that causes lumps, spots, and open sores.

Leper colony: a group of people living in the same area because they all have leprosy.

Mammal: one of a group of warm-blooded animals with a backbone and usually having hair.

Mineral: something in the earth, like diamond or coal, that needs to be dug out or mined.

Missionary: a person who carries on the work of a religious mission, often in a foreign country.

Plantations: large farms where slaves worked.

Polynesian: people from a large group of islands in the central Pacific Ocean.

Port city: a city where boats drop off or pick up cargo.

Symphony orchestra: a group of musicians playing many different instruments for an audience at a concert.

Tourism: tourists and all the business they bring to a place.

Tourist: a person traveling for pleasure.

Tropical: warm regions near the equator.

Volcano: an opening in the earth's crust through which steam, ashes, and lava are sometimes forced.

Internet Sites

Internet Island
http://www.hisurf.com
Bring your surfboard to Hawaii's virtual island! Learn the Hawaiian Language and discover Hawaiian local's favorite recipies.

Hawai'i Resource Library
http://hawaii-shopping.com/~sammonet/hrlhome.html
Hawaiian History, Culture, Art, Myths, Legal Documents, Photos, Ethnoarchaeology, Genealogies, Religion, Biology, Biographies, Opinions, & much more.

Planet Hawaii
http://planet-hawaii.com
On Planet Hawaii, the best of Hawaii is yours to experience in a web site intended to copy the islands themselves. If you're planning on visiting Hawaii, you might start with a trip to Planet Hawaii where you'll find a wealth of information and photos from all five of the major Hawaiian Islands. Planet Hawaii also features sections devoted entirely to business, culture, and publishing. In addition, there's the Hawaiian Eye, a live video camera trained on an island landmark.

These sites are subject to change. Go to your favorite search engine and type in Hawaii for more sites.

PASS IT ON

Tell Others Something Special About Your State

To educate readers around the country, pass on interesting tips, places to see, history, and little unknown facts about the state you live in. We want to hear from you!

To get posted on ABDO & Daughters website E-mail us at "mystate@abdopub.com"

Index